The *complete* guide to SCRAPBOOKING

*j*ILL HAGLUND

Scrapbooks push albums into a new dimension. By mixing elements of photos, art, memorabilia and writing you can showcase the highlights of your life the way you want. Some make your sides bend in laughter; others make your eyes well with tears. Whether it's a napkin from your first date with 'the one,' hospital tags from your newborn, pressed autumn leaves or renderings of your visit to Venice, scrapbooks are ideal for the preservation of your most precious items.

Exposures, Winter 1998

THE *complete* GUIDE TO
SCRAPBOOKING

JILL HAGLUND

The Complete Guide to Scrapbooking
ISBN: 1-891898-00-0
Copyright 1998 TweetyJill Publications

This book was designed and produced by TweetyJill Publications
P.O. Box 5824, Bee Ridge Road, Suite #412, Sarasota, FL 34233 800.595.5497

Editor: Kerry Arquette
Design Coordinator: Susha Roberts
Typist: Heidi Thomas

Photo Credits
Front Cover: Photography; Sean Kernan, Sean Kernan, Inc.
Back Cover: Photography; Nan Wasson, Heintz Wasson, Inc.
          Art Direction; Susan Caldwell
Title Pages: Photography; Sean Kernan, Sean Kernan, Inc.
Pages 14, 30 and 53, Photography; Nan Wasson, Heintz Wasson, Inc.
          Art Direction; Susan Caldwell
Pages ii, 8 (bottom) and 77: Photography; Michael Heintz, Heintz Wasson, Inc.
          Art Direction; Susan Caldwell
Pages 8 (top), 9, 59, and 79: Photography; Sean Kernan, Sean Kernan, Inc.
Pages 47, 51 and 102: Art Director/Designer; Michael Ostro, Ostro Design
          Photography; Lanny Nagler
Pages 6 and 27: Photography; Christopher Darling Photography
All other photos: Photography; Mike Everson, Dick Dickinson Photography

First Edition - Febuary, 1998
Second Edition - May, 1998

Printed in the United States of America by Central Florida Press

fROM THE AUTHOR

My passion for scrapbooking was born many years ago. I still remember painstakingly placing photos of my high school heartthrob in an old magnetic album. My affection for that boyfriend faded even before the photos did, so their deterioration was no great loss. With the resilience of the young, I went on to other loves and eventually found and married a man who owns my heart forever. We've shared wonderful times together and with family and friends, many of them documented by snapshots. It was important to me that these photos didn't fade or crack. I wanted to preserve and display them so that our life experiences and joys would be remembered. So, I began exploring the wonderful world of scrapbooking.

My interest in scrapbooking led me to a job as a scrapbooking consultant with an organization that provides instruction and products to scrapbookers. While I'm no longer with the company, I continue to encourage others to create memory albums through my job as an independent consultant, speaker and designer. I continue to share the scrapbooking tips, tools and tricks that I've developed over the years.

This book fulfills my dream of reaching a wide audience and, hopefully, encouraging readers to take their photos out of boxes and put them into albums. Albums are personal memory books and are a legacy we can hand on to future generations. They're a piece of us that never dies.

Jill Haglund

tABLE OF CONTENTS

introduction 1

paper, products & tools 7

tips, terms & techniques 15

project ideas 31

resource guide 100

PHOTO COURTESY FISKARS®

*t*HANKS

IT TOOK A REAL TEAM TO BRING THIS DREAM TO THESE PAGES. SPECIAL THANKS GO TO:

My children, Lindsay, Matthew and Jason, who contributed poems and artwork to this book and continue to be the focus of many of my sweetest memories.

My husband, Rob, who never gives up on me, always believes in me and takes up the slack at home.

Dianne Frailing, scrapbook advocate and my personal inspiration.

Karen Wiessner, my truest, bluest friend, fellow scrapbooker and sister-in-law who encouraged me and worked beside me to the end.

Michele Gerbrandt of Satellite Publishing, founder and publisher of *Memory Makers*® magazine, for her guidance and friendship.

My friend-in-the-industry, Peter Dunn, for his encouragement.

Lindsay Ostrom, author of *Creative Lettering* and *LMNOP More Creative Lettering With Lindsay*, for her contributions to this project.

Canson®, Fiskars®, C-Thru-Ruler®, McGill®, and other manufacturers for donating their outstanding products and photos.

Kerry Arquette, my editor, who touches words and turns them into magic. Without her talents this book would never have made its way to print.

Susha Roberts, my graphic designer, whose outstanding talents and technical skills transformed all of our efforts into a work of art.

Deborah Mock, my copy editor. Her sharp eye put the finishing touches on the package.

Heidi Thomas, typist, friend and reader of illegible writing.

To Lindy and Photocrop, for their prayers.

To my father-in-law Gordon, for his support and encouragement.

To my mother-in-law Marilyn, for her design expertise and special touch with styling the photo shoot.

This project has been completely orchestrated by our Lord's divine intervention in every phase along the way. It's been miracle after miracle, but then again...that's God! So, thanks, Dear Lord!

*T*his book is dedicated to my husband, Rob, our children, Lindsay, Matthew and Jason; and all my friends and colleagues who are committed to keeping memories alive.

*A*N INTRODUCTION
to scrapbooking

A scrapbook is one of the simplest and most basic records of life. It does not pretend to be history yet in its pages can be read a meaningful story. Into it goes— photographs of loved ones and favorite moments, treasured possessions, mementos of personal events (big and small) and fond recollections. To family and friends, the scrapbook is an introduction not only to daily events, but also to the spirit of the remembered past.

Max Lucado

IN ITS PUREST FORM, A SCRAPBOOK IS A CACHE FILLED WITH PRECIOUS, PRICELESS, ONE-OF-A-KIND TREASURES. THE MEMORIES within its pages are so distinct that no other person on the face of the earth could put together an identical book.

And yet, to some, the words scrapbook, heritage album or memory album conjure up images of imitation leather books filled with plastic-covered, sticky-pages on which photos are stacked like children's blocks. While these albums were a serviceable way to stash photos, they were void of charm and posed potential damage to the pictures.

In recent years, more and more people have been turning their backs on those no-effort scrapbooks. They want better for their photos and memories. They realize that, just as a museum director carefully chooses and designs a backdrop for priceless art, they too can enhance their personal photos by creating beautiful album-page backdrops.

Today's scrapbookers create whimsical, colorful pages using a plethora of products and tools available in many hobby and scrapbooking stores. Die cuts add variety; punches add balance; stickers add humor; all the products and tools make it easier for scrapbookers to put their personal imprint on their pages.

With products and purpose, all scrapbookers can turn out unique album pages. This book will lead beginners through the ABC's of putting together their first album. More experienced album enthusiasts will find inspiration in the project and theme pages.

The journey begins here, and the destinations are only as limited as your imagination.

on your way: getting started

Half the fun is getting there. It's true in life, and it's certainly true in scrapbooking! The process of putting together a memory album is almost as fulfilling as leafing through the finished pages. A scrapbooking session is a walk down Heritage Lane. The photos evoke memories of wonderful times and, if you're lucky, you'll relive events in your vivid past. Viewed that way, the job of sorting photos seems less tedious.

The hardest part of organizing may be dragging those boxes, packets and stacks of old photos out of closets and attics. This is a time to call in the troops. Not only can friends and family help cart and tote, they'll be immeasurably useful later on. Once the photos have been exposed to daylight, the task of organizing is straight forward:

zones

Set up shop on a large table or clear span of floor. Create "zones" 6-8" apart with sticky notes or labels. Each of these zones will be a category. Common categories include events, holidays, years, decades.

- Hint #1: Undated photos can be dated with a bit of sleuthing. Pay attention to clues, such as the ages of those portrayed, the buildings and furniture included in the shot, the year and model of any cars in the scene, etc.

- Hint #2: This is a great time to ask your "movers" and "toters" for their input.

store

Place completed piles of photos into separate, gallon-sized, plastic reclosable zipper bags or another storage container.

- Hint: Acid-free storage systems are available through the *Exposures* catalog. These affordable, photo-box files are safe, have reinforced edges and hold up to 1000 photographs. They also include an index. Store sorted photos in a cool, dry, dark place until you're ready to use them.

journaling

Once photos are safely taken care of, it's time to ferret out those stashes of the written word. Diaries, old letters, certificates, cards and memo pads are wonderful sources for material which will enhance albums.

While it may have been said that "a picture is worth a thousand words," a veteran albumist will tell you that a few well-chosen sentences can bring a photo to life, put it in perspective and add voice to an image. Adding text to a scrapbook page not only documents the events, it ensures that future readers will be able to view the photos in context.

Journaling in memory albums can be as straightforward and easy as adding dates and names, or it can be a poetic exercise, a flowing of the heart through a pen and onto the paper.

word-memories

If, like many, you have diligently kept photos but tossed written material, your job in photo journaling will be a bit more difficult. Difficult, but not necessarily unpleasant. The word-memories that support your photos will have to be your best recollections of events surrounding the shots.

"But, I have an absolutely terrible memory!" If that's you talking, relax. Techniques discussed in Robert M. Wendlinger's *Memory Triggering Book* can jump start your trip down memory lane. Wendlinger suggests creating maps of neighborhoods, streets, stores, playgrounds, schools and other areas pertinent to your past. Once the broad stroke map is completed, focus in. Create, for example, a floor plan of the school. Pencil in classrooms. Put down desk placements and designate blackboard walls, etc. Do the same for all important structures on the map.

The process of laying down the physical environment will trigger a wealth of memories. You'll suddenly remember Billy Ward tipping over his desk, which knocked over *your* desk, which created a domino of up-turned students. You'll recall that Mrs. Briggs was sick on picture-taking day, and that's why the substitute, a total stranger, appears in your class shot. Once the floodgates are open the "I remember when's..." will flow.

As memories surface, record them on scratch paper and lay them aside for a few days. While the words rest, your mind will be dredging up more material. Add the new anecdotes to the old. Edit. Then commit them to album pages.

compensate with words

Words can compensate for a lack of photos. If a great family story is begging to be told, but an illustrative photo doesn't exist, make do with what you have. Go on and tell that story about grandpa starting school at age five because the teacher (worried about him sitting outside the classroom door, waiting for siblings) invited him to take a seat.

Then, use the only photo you have of grandpa as a child (taken when he was three), and label it. Future generations won't hold it against you as long as the story is meaningful.

When sorting, labeling and recording is done, you'll have a wealth of organized material to use. Don't feel as though you must find an album home for all the rich and wonderful pieces immediately. As your album library grows (and it will), each piece will find its place. Don't rush it. Remember, half the fun is getting there...

My precious, little darling, Jason. When I look at this photo of you, I remember how your cuddly, warm body nestled in my arms. I recall that special baby smell you had after a fresh bath and the way your skin felt like velvet. I couldn't help myself...I must have kissed you a hundred times each day during that first year of your life.

xxoo-Mommy–1996

Your photo journaling will flow from your heart when you reflect on certain times and memories. Photographs stir your senses–reflect on smells and the "touchy-feelies" involved during the time of the snapshot.

Die cuts help tell the story. The photo shows Dad at age three. The story is about his early grade-school memories. The scissors, apple and school-themed die cuts set the stage. Gold documentation is done with a metallic pen. Keep the look of the era with gold photo corners.

PAPER, PRODUCTS & TOOLS

Scrapbooks and photo albums have warmed more hearts...Than any bound book because it's your life and feelings between those covers...without a good album, much that is memorable in life is forgotten, damaged or lost.

Don Asleth, Clutters Last Stand

THE BELOVED FACES OF YOUR ANCESTORS ARE BARELY DISCERNIBLE. THEY STARE BACK AT YOU FROM CRACKED PHOTOS, THEIR "Sunday best" permanently yellowed by careless storage of the pictures. It's enough to make you weep. The good news is that precious pictures are no longer doomed to such a fate. With the right care and the right products, family photos can be stored safely for generations.

archival quality

why acid-free?

Yellowing, cracking, staining and general deterioration often occur when photos make contact with acidic paper–paper with a pH level below 7. This means that all album pages and any paper products used in archival albums should be acid-free.

To be truly archival, paper must also be lignin-free. Lignin, an organic substance that adds strength and stiffness to paper by binding fibers together, reacts with light and heat to produce alcohol and acids. These by-products cause paper to yellow and break down over time.

pvc

Another culprit in photo degeneration is polyvinyl chloride (PVC), a chemical present in the plastic page overlay in magnetic (peel, press and stick) albums. When sandwiched between PVC and acidic paper, photos discolor, yellow and adhere with a death grip to album pages. Adhered photos can sometimes be released by sliding dental floss back and forth between the picture and the page. Remount the freed photos in an acid-, lignin- and PVC-free environment.

True acid-free, lignin-free, PVC-free products are the only choice for conscientious scrapbookers. Don't be taken in by cellophane wrapping claims of "acid-free," "photo-safe," or "light-fast." Read the labels. Know what you're getting.

products

albums

They vary in size from 4" x 6" to 12" x 18". They vary in price from $6 to $175. Album covers range from beautifully-designed, durably-constructed, acid-free cardboards to Italian linen, ivory brocade or beautiful, colored leather grains. The right album is the one that fits both your bookshelf and your budget. Before buying, ask yourself: Does this album offer enough room for journaling? Can the

RIGHT
Albums are available in a variety of covers to fit all budgets. Consider this Italian-linen album with tooled leather spine for holding your extra-special labors of love.

BOTTOM
Spiral albums are ideal when you have just a few photographs to display.

OPPOSITE
This album, clad in ivory brocade, makes an inspired home for your nuptial memories.

pages be removed and re-sequenced? Will I be happier with a spiral-bound style? (See pages 8 and 9 for album samples.)

page protectors

These transparent sheaths slide over album pages to protect photos and artwork from fingerprints, smudges, spills, dirt, dust and general abrasion. Because the protectors seal on only three sides, photos can still "breathe."

paper

Paper comes in a spread of beautiful colors, textures, patterns and weights. Combine and layer paper for outstanding appearance on pages. Adhesive-backed paper is unique in that you can punch it or cut it with decorative scissors into strips or shapes and it will adhere without curling. Tearing paper is a unique effect for matting and framing or for creating sandy beaches and mountains.

RIGHT
Adhesive paper prevents fancy cuts from curling on your page. Decoratively stamp your die-cut shapes once in a while just for the fun of it.
BOTTOM
Create waves with torn paper for a more "natural" effect.

paper/die cuts

These pre-cut paper shapes are designed to enhance album pages by adding dimension, style and balance. They are sold individually or in theme-related packages. Die cuts can also add a whimsical frame to photos, or can be used as a palatte for journaling. Trace and enlarge, cut in half or use in multiples for a unique effect. Some are adhesive-backed which makes application a breeze.

adhesives

Acid-free adhesives come in a variety of forms. Tape dispensers are inexpensive, expedient ways to adhere photos to an album page. Simply expose a bit of tape, drag the dispenser across the photo and lift, leaving behind small pieces in each corner.

"Temporary" adhesives make it possible to lift and place photos numerous times before committing to a layout. Double-sided adhesive squares are simple alternatives to tape. Simply pull out, peel off the protective backing and stick.

Acid-free glue pens and wands are also popular choices.

pens

Look for acid-free, permanent, fade-proof, non-bleeding and waterproof pens. Good quality pen sets with multiple colors are available for under $17. Invest in an assortment of pens with varying tips to make it easier to add variety to page titles and photo journaling.

ABOVE
Punch shapes from adhesive-backed papers and layer onto die-cut shapes. Clip matted frames with Fiskars® corner edgers.

templates

These plastic or acrylic stencils are used to cut or "crop" your photographs into different shapes and sizes. They come in a wide variety of designs and sizes. There are even alphabet templates to aid in fancy lettering.

rulers

No longer simply for straight-edged inch-counting, these tools now come in a large assortment of unique, decorative-edged designs that can add oomph to any page. Decoratively-edged rulers are also available in colored, transparent plastic to make placement accuracy easier.

trimmers and straight-edge scissors

These nifty tools are the answer to straight-edge cropping. You can remove the perfect amount and the cuts will be consistently straight and accurate. While the scissors must be used with finesse, trimmers take much of the guess work out of cropping. They allow visibility while you measure and align paper and photos.

decorative scissors

Like their relatives, pinking shears, these scissors make it possible to cut a multitude of shapes and patterns along the edges of paper. Dozens of designs are available, and by combining them in a project, your possibilities are endless.

punches

Punches create mini die-cut shapes. They come in hundreds of designs and a multitude of sizes. Punches are available for cutting silhouettes, borders, corner patterns, shapes and much more. Mix printed papers and solids for a designer look. To make miniature shapes, use Punchline™ hand punches, available in dozens of styles. These tiny punched shapes are excellent for creating borders on frames.

circle cutters

With this faithful tool you can cut a perfect circle from either papers or photos every time. Circle cutters can also help you create beautiful circular photo frames.

crimper

This nifty tool adds texture to paper. It adds variety, and helps create dimension for your punched (or cut) paper leaves, water, trees and more.

storage

Tools need a proper home in order to stay organized and in clean, pristine condition. Plastic food containers, stackable baskets, sewing boxes and padded envelopes all work well. Leeco Industries® has a great organizer for scrapbooking tools called The Cropper Hopper™. It includes portable bins for transporting supplies.

The right tools will not only make your task easier, they will also open up horizons of possibilities. An investment in proper tools is an investment in the quality of your albums.

*t*IPS, TERMS & TECHNIQUES

punch art

In their simplest form, punches can add whimsy to album pages. But the wide variety of punches now available make it possible for punch artists to "push the envelope" and make complex punch-art creations. Begin with basic punches then cut pieces of "this" and glue them to pieces of "that." In doing so, you can turn basic shapes into characters and creatures with distinct personalities. By varying paper colors and textures, punched art grows dimension. Dedicated border punches, complex corner punches, silhouette punches and corner rounders expand the artist's possibilities. Check out Satellite Publishing's punch-art book *Punch Your Art Out* for unique punch ideas.

cropping

The term "cropping" means cutting a photograph either down in size or into a different shape. A template placed over a photo (for example: a balloon shape over birthday photo) can act as a guide for cropping. Before cropping, trace around the edge of the template with a wax pencil especially designed to be wiped clean. Then, cut along the wax lines.

Cropping photographs draws attention to the important subject within the picture. By cutting out extraneous images and dark or blurry parts of the photo, you can free up room on a page for other shots.

Never crop a historical photograph. Everything in the frame of the photo gives it value and dates it. Someday today's photos will be considered "historical" too, so don't crop out your home, cars or sentimental items which will anchor them in a time period.

matting

Add color and dimension to your cropped shape by mounting it onto coordinating colored papers. Whether free-handing the mat, or using a template, be sure to cut the backing slightly larger than the photo. One-half-inch of paper should peer beyond the photo edges once the photo has been adhered. Use decorative scissors, or layer two colors of paper for a special effect.

Consider using two identical templates in different sizes. Use the larger template to trace a shape from acid-free paper. Use the smaller template as a guide for cutting the photo. Attach the photo to the larger image.

templates and lettering

Templates can be used as guides for lettering as well as cutting. Place a template firmly against a page and color in, or trace the outline of the letters. Write your message tightly within the borders of the template. Once the message is complete, lift off the template and–like magic–your chronicling efforts have taken on the shape of the template!

ABOVE

Matting techniques: Make use of identically-shaped templates by using the different sizes to mount your photographs. First, cut paper mat from the large-sized template. Next, cut photo from the smaller template. Place the photo onto the large paper template shape.

Use rulers to make borders, and document inside the decorative edges.

Rubber stamps look three-dimensional when you add color and layer die cuts on top.

Double mat photos using paper in contrasting colors and use paper edgers or decorative scissors to make beautiful frames for your photos.

OPPOSITE

Get excited about achieving bright, artistic borders by using only three tools:

1. Cut 1" x 4," 12" x 3.5" and 12" x 3" paper "border strips." Use a straight-edged cutter or a decorative rotary blade; cut against an acrylic ruler. Use adhesive-backed colorful papers so cut designs will lie smoothly on your page.

2. Layer cut strips according to size, from widest to narrowest.

3. Add die cuts to layered paper strips to create your own unique custom page border. Make two for a double-page spread.

silhouette cropping

This cropping technique requires you to cut around figures appearing in the photo. Because this is a can't-undo proposition, be sure to use only duplicate photos. Go slowly and try to stay true to the outline of the person. A slip while navigating the subject's midsection and the person in the image may find himself somewhat thinner. While that proposition may be rather pleasant, slips around the head can result in pointy ears and missing noses.

cropping in

Not only can you "crop out" unwanted portions of photos, you can "crop in" people or objects that wouldn't normally appear. This technique, when coupled with silhouette cropping, offers enormous benefits when trying to put together multi-figured layouts. Consider cropping in missing members of large, family group photographs. Get a bit crazy and crop in ambiance–a palm tree here, a coconut tree there and your whole family can be transported to Aruba with only a flourish of scissors and a bit of adhesive.

beyond the straight-edge

Straight-edged photos can be dolled up with the help of some decorative scissors, a decorative ruler and edge punches. Use a corner rounder punch to finish the corners, or use a decorative corner rounder to add a punched design as well as a rounded or intricately-shaped corner to your photos. Mount your cropped photo as is, or stick it to a lace doily or a contrasting mat.

Another easy way to make long, straight cuts with pizzazz is to use the Fiskars® Rotary Blade™. This tool allows you to "roll" out a decorative edge in eight different designs. When used with a self-healing mat, it couldn't be easier.

A little book called *Rule-It-Up* will open your eyes to unique and very do-able border techniques and template designs.

embossing

Embossing is sometimes done with a light box–available at office supply and auto stores. Try embossing using a decorative ruler. In order to do this, place ruler on the light box, and set the paper or page on top of the ruler. After aligning paper and ruler in the desired position, trace the ruler design with stylus. The end product is elegant; especially suited for special portraits, wedding and baby photo layouts. Ribbons or bows can be added to embossed ovals for a classic look. (For more embossing ideas see "rubber stamping" on page 22.)

two-page spreads

Don't get bogged down in a one-page-only mind-set. Two-page spreads are a wonderful alternative that allow you to use twice as many photos and make twice as much impact.

Consider a double-page spread if you have more good photos than you know what to do with, are dealing with a particularly special topic, or if you are trying to incorporate a special portrait shot. The pages on double-spreads are tied together by theme, color, topic and style. Be consistent.

balance

Trying to explain balance is a bit like trying to describe the flavor of an orange. It's one of those things you may find difficult to put into words. In scrapbooking, "balance" means to equalize in weight, form, color, proportion, importance and value specific photographs on a page. Good album pages balance large or dark photos with smaller or lighter photos. Two-page spreads must also be balanced against each other in order to be pleasing. While balancing comes naturally to some, others may benefit from reading *Core Composition*, available through Apple of Your Eye©. This book delves into the issues of balance and makes the weighing easier.

journaling

Journaling brings deeper meaning to scrapbook photos. It supplies important information which may seem obvious now, but won't be as obvious in years to come. Journaling can go well beyond just recording the mundane facts, it can wrap the photos in emotion.

Too many people are afraid of writing. What nonsense! Writing is really just talking through a pen. So, when journaling, try to block out the memory of your old English teacher's voice. Forget the rules of grammar, sentence structure and punctuation. Let the words flow from your heart.

What should you write about? Give basic information including the year, place, names and ages of those portrayed. Then ask yourself: Why is this photo special? What happened before or after this photo was shot that's important? What smells, sounds and tastes does this photo bring to mind? What was said or done that was funny or sad at the time that this photo was taken? How did the people in this photo feel at that moment? How did I feel? How do I feel when I look at the photo now?

Just as everyone has her own way of speaking, everyone writes differently. Eventually, you'll develop a style that feels good and flows from within.

As in writing, scrapbookers develop their own styles. It doesn't happen overnight, but over time and through experimentation you will find a style that is uniquely your own.Then your albums will be a window for others to celebrate the world as seen through your eyes.

Advanced Techniques for Scrapbooking

Color Wheel

Scrapbooks stir both our emotional and visual senses. Our visual sense is impacted strongly by color. Brain studies show that color arouses emotions ranging from tranquillity to aggression. You can use the power of color to help communicate mood in your scrapbook page layouts. An understanding of color usage will give you confidence to step out and try different color combinations.

A color wheel is an artistic reference that illustrates color relationships. Using a basic color wheel, you can see which colors best coordinate when selecting matting papers, die cuts, stickers or punch art. The color wheel will also guide you toward complimentary and appropriate contrast colors to use with color photos or memorabilia.

To find the complimentary color, begin by locating on the color wheel the color with which you're working. Then, simply cross directly over the color wheel to find its complimentary color. This complimentary color will make your photos jump off the page. Complimentary colors include:

Red and green

Yellow and purple

Blue and orange

Blue-violet and yellow-orange

Blue-green and red-orange

Analogous colors, those that are adjacent to each other on the color wheel, give a pleasant, harmonious, soothing look to a snapshot grouping.

Analogous colors include:

Green, blue-green and blue

---

color matters

Yellow is the color of:
Sunshine,
Soft sand on the beach,
A yolk in an egg
Baby chicks on Easter,
Daffodils,
Buttercups,
And sunflowers,
Part of the rainbow,
A ripe banana,
Lemonade on a summer's day,
A frozen Popsicle,
A canary in a tree,
A tennis ball!

Lindsay Haglund
Age 8

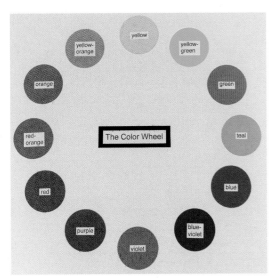

Red-orange, yellow and orange

Blue, blue-violet and violet

Strongly consider using analogous color when working with "busy" photos. They will steer you away from a cluttered look.

Aggressive colors such as red-orange, yellow and orange are good choices to enhance fall, harvest and Thanksgiving photographs. The cool receding colors such as blue, blue-violet and purple are good choices for matting snow and winter scene pictures.

Complimenting colors are located on the color wheel by locating the two colors on either side of your chosen color's "opposite." These colors make good choices for many types of album pages.

The triad principle is yet another design technique for color coordination. The triad is defined as any three colors on the color wheel equally spaced apart. These colors include the primaries of red-blue-yellow, as well as orange-purple-green.

Color wheels with rotating discs are available at fine art stores. These nifty tools are an investment that will help you light up your album pages.

- Hint# 1: Watch color selection
  Lighten up dark or subdued photos with brightly colored mattings.
  Be careful when mixing pastels with primary colored paper. Combine shades and tones only if they coordinate well.

- Hint# 2: Color generates emotions
  Blue–stability, security
  Red–anger, excitement
  Yellow–warm, flashy

The ABC's of Creative Lettering *and* LMNOP, More Creative Lettering by Lindsay *come highly recommended as great recources for scrapbookers who wish to enhance their lettering skills. The fun never stops once you start trying new lettering styles. Lindsay makes it easy…as easy as A-B-C! Zig™ markers has a wide variety of pen tips to play with.*

Rose

Button

Sweet

Licker Stix

Love

JILL ABC

Bell Bottom

LMNOP

m.o.r.e
creative lettering
with Lindsay

By Lindsay Ostrom & Friends '98

sticker art

Stickers are the last, but not the least, item to add to your page design. If stickers are added before the photo layout and journaling is completed, they invariably end up being stuck exactly where you wanted to write.

There are dozens of sticker companies and thousands of sticker designs to choose from. Carefully consider how many stickers you want to use and exactly where they should be placed before going hog wild.

Stickers come in a slew of different sizes. Small stickers make great "bullet points" in informal journaling. They also make wonderful, quick and easy borders.

- Hint #1: Sticker tips
  Never adhere a sticker to a photograph.
- Hint #2: Add stickers last
  Make stickers the last item added to your finished page (unless they're being used for border or corner treatments, or in a special "boxed" design).

rubber stamping

The introduction of safe pigment ink pads brought scrapbookers and stamp enthusiasts together in a big way! Now, scrapbookers are able to take advantage of the hundreds of stamp designs sold in craft, fine art and hobby stores. Used in combination with the numerous ink pad colors, stamp artists are now able to wield their art in unlimited designs.

These simple tools, consisting of an engraved or carved rubber image mounted on a wood block, can bring a lot to album pages. But, when a rubber stamp image is embossed, it really comes to life.

Embossing with rubber stamps raises the image from the paper or page. To emboss:

- Stamp your image using a special embossing pad and ink.

- Select a colored embossing powder. Sprinkle the powder over the wet, inked image.

- Shake off the excess powder.

- Apply heat evenly, keeping the image three to four inches away from the heat source.

Within seconds, a beautiful, colored image surfaces. Rubber stamp images embossed on beautiful colors of paper look like a work of art.

lettering

Lettering adds a highly personal element to a scrapbook. Even if your elementary teachers despaired over your handwriting, you can learn to embellish your scrapbook pages with the stroke of a pen. There are many good lettering books on the market including Lindsay Ostrom's *The ABC's of Creative Lettering*. This volume has great suggestions that allow you to get the most from pen tips, along with some creative lettering ideas.

Other great lettering books for your library include *Lettering and Liking It* and *Lettering and Liking It, Too*, both by author Sandy Tyson. Within these volumes you'll find both lettering tips and unique ideas for photo titling.

A time investment in mastering lettering techniques will pay off in beautiful, one-of-a-kind album pages. The way you slant your letters, the force you apply to the pen, the script you choose are the voice that you project to future generations.

cute quotes and sayings

Pick up some books of classic quotations for page title ideas. The three-volume set *425 Heartwarmin'* *Expressions* has quips and quotes that add warmth and humor to pages and is a good first purchase for your collection The books are divided topically, for easy reference.

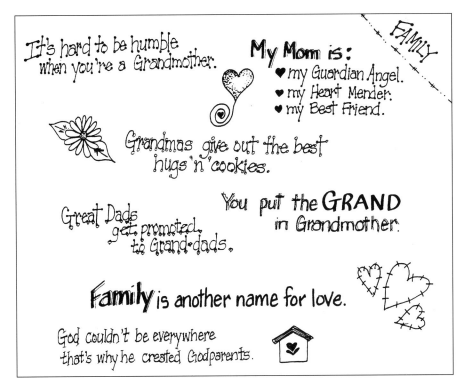

memorabilia display

Memorabilia can be displayed in a variety of ways:

- As long as photographs are not touching memorabilia, you can permanently mount directly on the page.

- Use photo corners in if you wish to be able to easily remove the memorabilia at a later time. Consider using photo corners for one-of-a-kind photos so they can be removed for reprints at a later date.

- Bulky memorabilia, such as hospital bracelets and locks of ribbon-tied hair, can be placed in a small plastic mylar sleeve to accomodate precious objects and keep the page surface smooth.

- For memorabilia collections such as postcards or brochures, use pocket pages.

- Special storage pages are available to make easy viewing of certificates and double-sided documents.

ABOVE

Decorative stencil rulers by Cut-It-Up™ do a double duty, adding fancy borders and small creative shapes to your layout. Instructions in Rule-It-Up *gives hundreds of ideas for using these snappy little tools.*

OPPOSITE

TOP

Embossing white paper adds elegance to page layouts. Place your stencil on a light box and put your page on top of the stencil. Use a stylus to imprint the design.

BOTTOM

Special techniques layer a gold-embossed die cut onto colored paper. Use Fiskars™ corner edgers to clip the corners before matting onto lace doily. Punch all three layers with an oval Punchline™ punch and thread ribbon through top portion. Use a rotary trimmer to make Victorian border cuts.

Use your circle cutter or compass to cut three sizes of circles from two coordinating colors. Emboss circles in gold with a delicate design, such as this stamp by Inkadinkadoo™. Victorian decopage flowers add elegance and a finishing touch.

custom paper cutting

Cutting your own custom die cuts from acid-free paper allows you to design special, original page layouts. If needed, use a self-healing mat board and craft knife to cut out the inside details you can't reach with a scissor.

taking better pictures

Photos are the bread and butter of any scrapbook. A good photo makes an albumist's job easy. It begs to fill a page and requires little embellishment.

Photography is an art. It takes knowlege and practice to master. Here are some tips that will help move you along from fledgling to soaring photographer.

- FOCUS ON THE SUBJECT
  Make your subject the focus of your shot. Close-ups make a big impact.

- ELIMINATE DISTRACTIONS
  Zoom in or move in on the subject to eliminate distracting backgrounds. This cuts down on later cropping.

- SHOOT AT EYE LEVEL
  Shots taken at eye level capture expressions and create emotional closeness. Kneel down or sit down when photographing children in order to gain this intimate perspective.

- CATCH THE ACTION
  Don't always stop to pose your subject. Catch the action while it's happening; while feet are flying and hair is whipping.

- CHOOSE FILM WISELY
  Low light action shots and bright sunlight all require different film speeds or ASA (film speed written by the American Standards Association). Read up on film qualities and then read the box labels before buying. Keep a variety of film on hand.

- FIND THE ANGLE
  Alter the angle to eliminate background distraction and add variation.

- STEADY YOUR CAMERA
  Don't let camera movement blur your shots. Press your camera tightly to your forehead to hold your camera steady. Hold your breath. Click.

- CARE FOR EQUIPMENT
  Clean your lens often. Store it carefully to prevent scratching.

- WATCH OUT
  Keep fingers and camera straps away from front of viewfinder.

- BANISH RED-EYE
  Prevent red-eye by angling your camera slightly away from subject or use a bounced light.

Dry paper embossing adds elegance and grace to paper. You can emboss directly onto your scrapbook page using brass template border designs and sayings. Or you can emboss onto acid-free paper to enable you to layer colors, adding depth and richness to your layout. Another technique is embossing directly onto die cut shapes. Adhesive-backed shapes work especially well, just peel and adhere your custom embossed shape to your page. See p.18 for additional information.

STEP 1

Gather your brass templates and stylus tool. Turn on your lightbox and line up your scrapbook page, paper or die cut shape directly over the brass template you choose. Remember to always work on the reverse side of your page, paper or die cut, so the embossed image will be on the proper side. Place the template as you'd like it to appear in your page layout– such as border, center top, top right. Make sure it is exactly like you want it before proceeding. The light makes it easy to view the anticipated layout through light-colored paper.

STEP 2

Rub the area on the page, paper or die cut you have chosen for embossing with a crumpled piece of wax paper. This technique helps your stylus tool glide around the design easier.

STEP 3

Press the stylus tool firmly into the edges of the design and trace completely. Double check to see that all parts of the template are traced before you remove it from the light box.

CREATIVE IDEAS FOR DECORATIVE RULERS

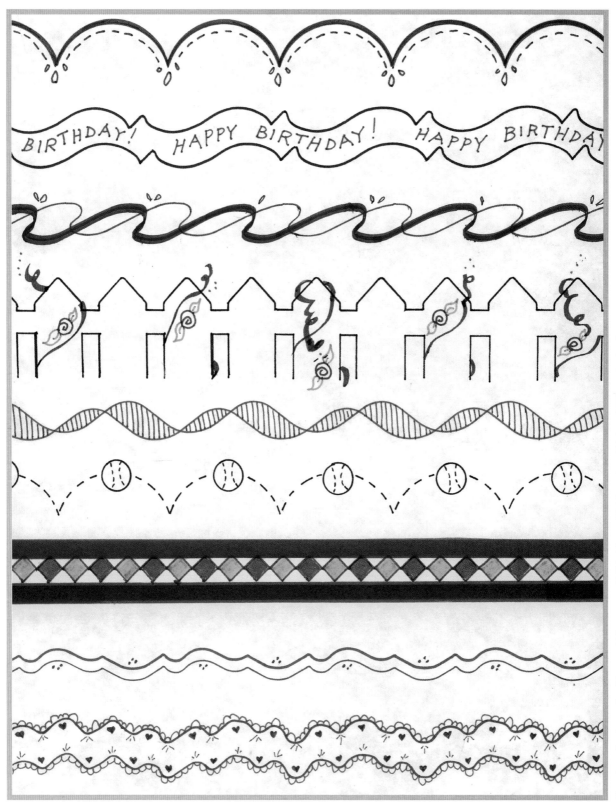

BIRTHDAY! HAPPY BIRTHDAY! HAPPY BIRTHDAY

Border designs by Karen Wiessner. Déjà Views™ View-lers™ by C-Thru Ruler®.

Team up Canson's® beautiful acid-free papers and
a circle cutter for creative page layouts.

Project Ideas

Memories

From Grandma's home-baked cookies
And my Mother's apple pie,
To my child's mischievous antics done
With a twinkle in his eye.

The past to well remember
With memories of such pleasures.
To relive those special moments
Is something I dearly treasure.

In today's fast-paced schedule of
Ballet, baseball and carpools,
I dedicate this precious time
With love to my priceless jewels.

To future generations that
Only God's eyes can see,
I place this book unto your care
From a memory keeper, that's ME!

Karen Wiessner

PROJECT 1

anniversary album

★★★

Once, in a time long ago, there lived a beautiful young girl who wanted, more than anything in the world, to fall in love and live happily ever after. One day, the man of her dreams walked into her life and straight into her arms. They wed, and their life was long and joyful. As with good fairy tales, the couple lived happily ever after.

You can record those many years of joyful memories, from wedding to children's births and on to the golden years, in an anniversary album.

Along with photos, allow each family member to contribute memories and feelings. It's more than just a tribute to longevity. It's a tribute to love and devotion.

how hard is it?
Each album has been rated to make pro-ject selection easier. Theme pages with five stars are more complex and require more time. With the right tools and determination, all scrapbookers can turn out their own version of these pages.

★	i can
★★	i can try
★★★	i can hope
★★★★	i can wish
★★★★★	i can dream

There is no more lovely, friendly and charming relationship, communion or company than a good marriage.

Martin Luther

Long after the honeymoon is over, you can transfer your wedding photographs to a photo-safe environment with acid-free products. Capture a classic look by matting photos on black and cream. Stenciling adds elegance to the page.

PROJECT 2

a child's autobiography album

★★★

It started in the eyes. There was a twinkle and then the corners crinkled. It spread to the lips and, little by little, that tiny face lit up like dawn creeping over the horizon. It was your child's first smile, and you'll never forget it. How strange to think that your son or daughter has no recollections of that special moment or other early experiences.

Help your child create her own album to introduce her to her past. It's a way of saying "This is who you were," and "This is who you are becoming."

On these pages, she can record the milestones of her life; those first steps she took, the first tooth she lost, the T-ball games and sleepovers. It's an album she will carry off to college along with your heart.

Author's note: This spread is from my niece Sarah's album, done by her own hands with a little help from Mom. Special memories of a mother-daughter mini-vacation to the Rocky Mountains to visit the Pieper Family. Teach your children to scrapbook at an early age, so they establish good photo preservation skills for life.

PROJECT 3

church youth album

★★

It's a place to pray and a place to play!

Churches, synagogues and other religious centers are no longer solemn places where patent leather Mary Janes, bow ties and white gloves are the dress code. More and more, the halls of religious institutions are filled with laughing children complete with tennis shoes and basketballs. They're there for junior choir practice, drama club, religious school, summer camp, fund-raisers and, of course, worship.

Capture those special memories in a church youth album. The faces of these special friends and special events will always remind your children of the joy, camaraderie and fulfillment within sacred walls.

Church youth activities such as camp can be a big part of your child's summer memories. Try cutting out letters for titles using dud or duplicate photos. Have you ever accidentally taken a photo of the leaf-strewn ground when attempting to shoot fall pumpkins? Use "oops" shots as paper from which to cut out titles.
Scissors technique: Make a lake from blue paper using decorative scissors and let a fish sticker swim in it. Punched Evergreen trees spread across the page to give an outdoor feeling.

*P*ROJECT 4

college memories, fraternity/sorority album

★★

Who would have thought that those gum wrappers, ticket
stubs, napkins and class doodles would ever seem important?

Now, they represent a carefree time in your life when childhood was behind you and adulthood before you. "Fun"
seemed to be the password of the day, and boy, did you
embrace it!

Relive those good times with a college album. Think hard,
and you may be able to remember those fraternity or sorority
songs, the old college motto and the name of the football
quarterback you dated (or envied).

Go wild with school colors. Cut out shapes of the school's
mascot and roll in spirit and nostalgia.

I had a favorite teacher
When I was very small.
She taught me how to write my name,
And how to throw a ball.
She taught me all the alphabet,
From A right down to Z.
But most importantly of all,
She taught me to like me!

K. Mahrer

PROJECT 5

teacher gift album
★★

It was so scary!

The hallways seemed to go on forever. There were millions of kids in millions of thudding shoes. Their footsteps echoed off the walls like a giant's brigade. And then you found your classroom, and, inside, a desk with your name on it!

And your teacher said, "I'm so excited to meet you, and so happy you're in my class!" And she smiled. Suddenly, school didn't seem like such a scary place at all!

You'll never forget that teacher, or the teachers who followed. Now, your child's teacher is wrapping her in the same kind of warm fuzzies that you enjoyed all those years ago. Say, "Thank you" by presenting her with a teacher gift album.

Gather memorabilia and photographs of school events, such as field trips, programs, plays and concerts, along with snapshots of teachers and students at work and play. Include a photo of the school.

While an apple makes a lovely gift, this album will find a favored spot on both the teacher's desk and in her heart.

PROJECT 6

cookbook scrapbook album
★★

It sounded gross! Mayonnaise cake! Yuck!

But Grandma insisted on making it anyway, and when it was iced and on the table, you couldn't tell there was a bit of mayonnaise in it! It was rich and fluffy and totally yum, and it became a family favorite. Preserve those memories with a cookbook scrapbook album.

Include your special recipes and photos of family members hard at work either whipping up holiday cookies or washing up mixing bowls. Don't forget to include photos of those batter-smeared children's faces that are sweeter than the richest pie.

Remember the first time your toddler cracked an egg? Recall the time the electric beater became possessed and sprayed batter all over the kitchen walls? Write it all down so your little chefs-to-be can remember some of life's warmest experiences.

Cooking is like love. It should be entered into with abandon or not at all.
Harriet Van Horne

Some of life's most treasured hours are those spent in the kitchen with children. Featuring the gingerbread houses in an album makes them feel appreciated. Don't forget to include favorite family recipes in your album. Keep your camera nearby during these special cooking sessions.

PROJECT 7

church scrapbook album

★

Home is where the heart is, and for many, their church, synagogue, mosque or temple is truly home. It's a place to worship, yes, but also a place to meet friends, to eat, to work and to play.

Within a church scrapbook album, you'll find a home for all those wonderful photos of your men and women's ministries in action. This is a place for photos of ladies teas, community outreach and singles group events, Bible studies, dinners, picnics, holiday celebrations and special programs.

What a wonderful way to share information about your religious institution with new members! What a wonderful way to celebrate the blessings of friends and experiences you've received!

I will sing of the Lord's great love forever;
with my mouth I will make your faithfulness known through all generations.
Psalm 89:1

Gospel concerts, such as this one by "The Faithful Four," make great photos and are wonderful pages to add to your church album. Make your own filmstrip using a rectangular-shaped Punchline™ punch. Musical die cuts and stars add flair. The triad color wheel combination (see the color wheel on page 20) of red, blue and yellow make the pages bright and exciting.

PROJECT 8

decade album

★

It seemed to pass in a frantic blur.

There were thousands of runs to the grocery store, zillions of meals to prepare and more loads of laundry than you can remember. There were children to wash and watch and snuggle. There were people who needed your care and people who wanted your company. There were errands to run. And there were soccer games...oh, so many soccer games to cheer on!

Somehow, the years just got away from you and now you're staring at boxes and boxes of photos. You haven't the energy or the time to tackle a complicated scrapbooking project. What should you do?

A decade album is the answer to your prayers. This broad-stroke book can be filled randomly with photos that fall within a ten-year span. Your photos will have a safe home and you'll still have time to kick around a ball with your kids.

Therefore all seasons shall be sweet to thee,
Whether the summer clothe the gentle earth
With greenness, or the redbreast sit and sing
Betwixt the tufts of snow on the bare branch.
Samuel Taylor Coleridge

Easy as 1,2,3 or two by two! Just cut out mats for photos, using decorative scissors. Jumbo scalloped scissors give the giraffe a mane. Add cutouts from an amusement park brochure to enhance the page layout. Yes, it has acid, but if acidic memorabilia does not touch the photos, you're safe. Add a page protector to keep photos and memorabilia from coming in contact once the album is closed.

PROJECT 9

old grade-school memories album
★★★

It all started with Mrs. Briggs and you'll never forget her.

She was magic. She led you into wonderful worlds where dragons talked, plucky heroines had great adventures and everyone lived happily ever after. She taught you that math made sense, that friends should be kind, and that there's a place in every day for milk and cookies.

Other teachers followed, each sharing the best of their knowledge. Commemorate those teachers and those special school days with a grade school memories album.

Dig up class pictures and yearbooks. Uncover secret notes, snapshots and report cards. A visit to your local library may result in clippings about events that took place at your school or within your community.

Enrich your album by contacting old friends. (The internet people-search sites are a good place to start. Or, track them down through other friends or family.) Ask them to write a few paragraphs about their memories of those elementary school years you shared.

Look in your attic and closets for photos and memorabilia from your old grade-school days. Check with your parents, relatives or grade-school friends for additional mementos. Don't forget to include all those after-school activities that were such a part of your life.

PROJECT 10

traditional family album

★

A round of Monopoly; a Sunday afternoon driveway game of basketball; a before-bed session of reading and snuggles. These are the moments of which family life is made.

While the one-of-a-kind vacations to exotic places may seem important at the time, it's the day-to-day events that will sit most heavily in your memory.

Capture them on film. Record them in words, and set them down as they unfold in a traditional family album. This book will be as comfortable and familiar as a well-worn teddy bear or a favorite easy chair. Settle in and enjoy.

You have the special privelege of providing a link to that heritage for oncoming generations. Write about yesterday. Write about today, which will be history tomorrow.

Lois Daniel

A typical scene...kids playing dress-up. Sticker borders tell the story and are easy to apply. When doing a border, apply stickers before snapshots.

PROJECT 11

heritage album

★★★★

What did he love about her the most?

Was it the way her hair struggled free from that ivory comb, or the way the very top button on those tiny boots refused to stay closed? What did she love about him the most? Was it that funny mustache, twisted like a barber's pole or the jaunty way his hat sat on his head?

Couple old photos with family stories (Older family members love sharing "I-remember-when" sagas. Take a tape recorder along when visiting.) Birth certificates and newspaper clippings help a family history album to free the past and live once again.

The next thing most like living one's life over again seems to be the recollection of that life, and to make that recollection as durable as possible by putting it down in writing.
Ben Franklin

PROJECT 12

proud grandparents album

★

Mothers say, "Brush your teeth. Do Your homework. Set the table." Grandparents say, "Sit on my knee and I'll tell you a story!"

Fathers say, "Take out the trash. We've got errands to run. Time for a haircut." Grandparents say, "It's time for a picnic! It's time for a snuggle! It's time to make cookies!"

The special relationship between grandparents and grandchildren is what makes a proud grandparents album so special.

This book, filled with "the best and brightest kids in the world–my grandkids!" is just perfect for display on a coffee table. But, more likely, it will be carried around in a bag, or purse, so consider making it in a smaller size.

After all, your special grandparents will want to be prepared for that moment when someone unsuspectingly asks, "So…how are those grandkids of yours, anyway? What are they up to these days?"

What faces! They were made for kissing, squeezing and showing off. Make your favorite grandparent an album filled with grinning images of their favorite kids.

PROJECT 13

a child's life album

★★

Like a child learning to walk, albums move forward step by cautious step.

A child's album gently, but firmly takes shape under loving hands. Begin, if you can, with your baby's birth. Along with those bald-headed hospital photos, include a copy of your newborn's birth certificate and hospital bracelet.

Move forward in time, capturing the special first smile, the speedy crawler and proud toddler. Capture your child's milestones and set down in words the way your heart sang at your first glimpse of her precious face; the way your heart caught in your throat the day she stepped off on her own.

If you could lay love down on a page, this is where it would belong.

*Babies are bits of stardust blown
from the hand of God.*

Larry Barretto

Die cut letters are great for making names. Photos of handmade baptismal gowns, baby shoes and first stuffed animals start you on your way. Don't forget to document their significance and history.

PROJECT 14

man's career album
★★

At last! An answer to the age old question of what to get your husband or other special man in your life, for the next gift-giving occasion! A man's career album is a wonderful present, no matter what your man's profession. These albums often begin with mementos of a military stint. Include any photos of his military friends, as well as letters from home, postcards, invitations to military reunions and awards. Draw from the stories your husband has shared in order to journal his favorite experiences.

Move forward to chronicle your husband's work history, paying special attention to the positions that have brought him the most fulfillment and pride. Include memorabilia, certificates, letters, newspaper clippings and even logbooks, (if your special man has fulfilled soaring ambitions). While it's not possible to put an old trophy in this album, it is possible to include photos of those awards.

A man's career album is also a wonderful project for your husband to tackle on his own. Many men enjoy exploring the art of scrapbooking while working with professionally-related topics. This is a forum for them to write about their feelings surrounding their job choices, the relationships they developed while working and their goals.

A man who invests the time to put together a career album may find he's been bitten by the scrapbooking bug!

Gather together photos and memorabilia to create a career album. Begin with early remembrances such as a pilot's-first solo flight certificate. Continue through each advancement. This album rings with pride.

PROJECT 15

portfolio album
★★

A portfolio is an adult's Show-and-Tell.

It's a book filled with, "This is who I am," "This is where I've been," and "This is what I've done." Within a portfolio album you can place the best examples of your work, commendations, professional articles and any press coverage you may have attracted.

Unique design and that special dash a creativity set your professional album apart from the dozens of others which will pass across a potential employer's desk and beneath his eyes.

Long after the door has closed behind you, the interviewer will remember you as an applicant whose portfolio was as unique as the employee you are bound to be.

All are architects of Fate,
Working in these walls of Time;
Some with massive deeds and great,
Some with ornaments of rhyme.
Henry Wadsworth Longfellow

Use a classic album for displaying your portfolio.

We will tell the next generation the praise-worthy deeds of the Lord, His power, and the wonders He has done.

Psalm 78:4

PROJECT 16

christian heritage album
★★

Spiritual values are the most important gift we can give our children.

What a precious heirloom for them to share with future generations! A christian heritage album is a testimonial to beliefs that will last the test of time. Those beliefs and faith bind the pages together.

Along with favorite photos of church-related events, you can include testimonials from family members and Bible verses. Like salvation, these verses are there for those who seek:

Thou hast been my God from my mother's womb. Psalm 22:10 (Photos of young children)

I praise You because I am fearfully and wonderfully made. Psalm 139:13

Man looks outward at appearance, but the Lord looks at the heart. Samuel 16:7 (Photos of innocent children)

God created the heavens and the earth. Genesis 1:1 (Photos of nature)

His name is holy from one generation to another. Luke 1:50 (Family photos, grandparents with children)

Whatever your hand finds to do, do it with your might. Ecclesiastes 9:10 (Youth doing crafts in church or Sunday School activities)

A, B, C, D, E, F,G.
H, I, J, K, L, M, N, O, P!
Q, R, S, and T, U, V,
W, X ,and Y, and Z.
Now I know my ABC's.
Tell me what you think of me!
unknown

PROJECT 17

abc album

★

Start this album, and you'll soon have every child within helping distance clamoring to participate. Take advantage of this enthusiasm and the extra hands. It's a great way to grow the next generation of scrapbook enthusiasts.

Begin an ABC album by either making or purchasing each letter of the alphabet. Die cut shapes and sticker letters work well, or cut your own letter forms. Adhere a letter to each page, or create double-page spreads.

You have oodles of flexibility when selecting photos to appear beneath each letter heading, for example, a ski photo with Sarah in it could be placed on your S page, for "ski" or "snow" or "Sarah." But this photo could also appear on your A page for "Aspen," or on your W page for "winter fun."

This quick and easy project doesn't call for photo mounting. You can stick the pictures directly to the scrapbook pages.

Begin each photo's documentation with the letter of the page on which it falls. For example, that shot of Sarah, which appears on your S page, could read, "Sarah and I having a blast on our special vacation with our families in Snowmass, CO. BRRRRRR! What a letter-perfect project!

PROJECT 18

boy scout or girl scout album
★★

It was about much more than just cookie sales or fund raisers.

It was about working as a group, about learning to be a friend, about sharing your gifts and talents with each other. It was about hiking and arts and crafts and learning. It was about fun!

Save all those scouting experiences in a special Boy or Girl Scout album. Include photos of the wonderful (and sometimes wacky) events that made those scouting times so memorable. Here's where those photos of that great talent show belong, along with the camp pictures and visits to retirement homes.

Color copy and enlarge images of patches, scarves, badges, and the cover of the scouting manual. Include scouting awards and memorabilia. Don't forget to write down the scouting promise.

Then, think about throwing a party and inviting over all those fellow trail blazers for a hike down memory lane!

Camping photos, whether from Scout camp or summer camp experiences, look great among these trees. Use die cut shapes in multiples. Cut in half to create "woods." Trim cut adhesive-backed paper with decorative scissors to create a "lake." Photos of cousins hugging in excitement and anticipation of "no mom week," the camp sign and cabin-mates photo bring the scene to life.

PROJECT 19

seasonal album

★

When the days grow nippy and the night comes early, pull out your photos and tackle a seasonal album. This is an easy way to organize a plethora of shots. Just as there's a time for every season, there's a place for every photo.

Begin with those nippy-weather shots of your children turning the backyard into a flurry of snow angels and those photos of family ski trips.

Spring into pictures of the family garden being planted or festive colored-egg hunts.

Then warm up to summer shots of your little porpoises frolicking in turquoise pools, or of lemonade and orange-stained Popsicle faces.

Fall photos of apple picking and leaf fights, football games and Thanksgiving feasts follow.

Before you know it, you're back to winter and ready to begin another album!

Cutting the photo of a child racing to the finish at a Fourth of July picnic creates movement. The patriotic die cuts come in red, white and blue. Cut and interchange die cut shapes for a split-color effect. Sandy Tyson's Lettering and Liking It *helps with title design.*

Project 20

vacation and/or travel album
★★

Dear Grandma and Grandpa. We are on vakation! It is lots of fun! We drove forever and we saw lots of signs and lots of cows and lots of gas stations! Charlie threw up. He is better now, but Mom says he can't reed in the car any more. We are finally at the beach. The sand is mushy and the water is wet. Wish you were hear!
Love,
Mary (your granddaughter)
p.s. Don't forget to feed Spott

A family vacation album will allow you to live those great vacation days again and again.

Include maps, brochures, napkins from favorite eateries, pages from your travel log and names and addresses of new friends you met along the way.

Beg back those letters your children sent to their grandparents. They'll keep you chuckling long after your tans have faded.

After browsing through those photos of sun and surf, of mountains and meadows, of sparkling ski slopes, you'll find yourself browsing through travel brochures and planning future adventures.

When putting together a vacation album, whether it's from a trip to Grandma's in Minnesota or a two-week, once-in-a-lifetime stint in Europe, collect all the travel memorabilia you can. Examples: color copy your stamped passport pages, add your train tickets, map sections, emblems, patches, postcards, menus and postage stamps from the country or state you're visiting. Document your journey on a copied map, if possible, and include in your album.

*P*ROJECT 21

cruise album

★

Ahoy there, sailors! Don't let your memories of that terrific cruise slip over the horizon and fade from sight. Put together a special cruise album. You'll find yourself bobbing along on high spirits as you relive your vacation through this project.

Select the best of those photos of you sipping something wonderful beside the pool. Include the picture of your shipboard shuffleboard games and those evenings when you danced until dawn against a backdrop of too-blue-to-be-true ocean. Add postcards of your liner, the daily programs slipped under your door by your personal cabin attendent, menus and descriptions of off-ship excursions.

This album will make a big splash with friends and family.

*I must go down to the
seas again,
to the
lonely sea and the sky,
And all I ask is a tall ship,
and a star to steer
her by;*

John Masefield

Make a splash with a cruise album that brings back those carefree days of sun and fun.

PROJECT 22

christmas album

★

It's twinkling lights and gingerbread cookies. It's mistletoe and heart-felt carols. It's gifts and prayers and family. It's Christmas!

Over the years, your Christmas album will become as important a part of this special holiday as Santa, the tree and that beautiful candle-light service.

Family will enjoy leafing through the album and recalling those special Christmases in the past...the one when the puppy ate the fruitcake; the one when a very special grandma chose to give a very special ornament; the one when the tree was so big it brushed against the ceiling!

Make working on your Christmas album a part of the festivities and then set it on the coffee table for all to enjoy. What a gift for the whole family! What a celebration of the season! What a way to say....Happy Holidays!

*'Twas the night before Christmas,
When all through the house
Not a creature was stirring,
Not even a mouse.*

Clement C. Moore

For this Christmas layout, fold green paper in half and free-hand cut a tree shape. Cut tree and a star die cut in half to fit onto a two-page layout. Border pages with pen embellishments and stickers. Trim the tree with die-cut shapes, photos and stickers.

PROJECT 23

your child's school memories album

★★★

School days, school days, good old Golden Rule days! While your children may swear that those days of rulers, markers and erasers crept by with inchworm slowness, you know better. In a blink, your child changed from a gap-toothed kindergartner to a self-assured young graduate. What ever happened to all those years in between? A child's school memories album is a wonderful way to relive those growth-filled years.

A school album takes shape as the school years unfold. Into this book you can place copies of report cards, school pictures, teacher's names, favorite subjects, special artwork, certificates and school work. Document your child's physical growth by tracing his hand on an album page each year, using an acid-free pen. Then, record all the milestones that happened that year: the first two-wheel bike ride; the trip to the science museum; the big spelling bee; and that first sleepover.

What does he want to be when he grows up? What songs, movies, plays and books does he enjoy? What does he eat for breakfast? If he's a hot basketball player, make note of it, and include the names of friends.

Take the time to make this album special and you'll never regret it.

I watched them walk to the bus today
And couldn't help but ponder;
In a blink, it seems, the years go by,
But the images still linger.

Unknown

School days, enhanced with punched hand shapes from McGill™ work as a border. Create your own die cuts from acid-free paper (world, pencil, blackboard). Make a pocket page to hold grade cards and other memorabilia by using adhesive-backed paper. Remove the adhesive only from around the edges, about ¹/₂ inch on three sides; decorate with die cuts.

PROJECT 24

family reunion album
★★

Whether they traveled across the ocean, across the continent, or around the block, it's wonderful to see family members! Bringing them together at the same time and in the same place takes planning, faith and a whisper of divine intervention. Don't let the occasion pass without recording it in a family reunion album!

A family reunion album is not only a wonderful record, it's also a terrific reunion project! Ask attendees to bring along photographs, favorite recipes and old reunion invitations. Hand out disposable cameras, set others on picnic tables, and encourage everyone to click away. Lay out the album and acid-free pens and see to it that everyone takes a minute to record his thoughts, feelings and memories. When putting together your album include a current invitation, a list of those invited and note those who made it. Go ahead and try for a family portrait, but don't become frantic if you can't get everyone to stand still. Just make sure you have individual photos. Include the person's name, birthday and some fun information about his or her hobbies and favorite foods.

Your reunion album will be the centerpiece of next year's reunion dinner!

A man travels the world over in search of what he needs and returns home to find it.

George Moore

Family reunion albums include old and new photos spread across generations. Add to it each time you get together. Paper becomes so much more when you combine, cut, layer and emboss with rubber stamps. Canson-Talens (known in the U.S. as Canson), a 500-year-old paper mill in France, manufactures the cream of the crop. The beautiful texture makes it especially adaptable to rubber-stamped, embossed images. Layering gives depth to matting. Gold corners and lettering add a timeless finishing touch.

PROJECT 25

pet album

★★

She's your companion. She's your children's nanny. She's your chief kitchen-spill cleaner-upper. She's your friend. She's your dog (or cat or hamster or ferret).

No matter what kind of pet you have, she's definitely a member of the family. Capture her warm, funny, quirky personality in the pages of a pet album.

Include all your wonderful photos: the one with your five-year-old taking your bonnet-bedecked kitty for a ride in the doll's buggy.

Build on this album and you'll be able to see the evolution of body-wagging puppy to sleek and trim dog, or purring kitten to independent cat.

How much is that doggy in the window?
The one with the waggly tail?
How much is that doggy in the window?
I do hope that doggy's for sale!

Unknown

PROJECT 26

travel log album

★★

Chronicle your travels–especially that long, extended stay in Italy, or that stint as a foreign exchange student to Venezuela.

Use a journal-style album with snapshots simply adhered to the page. No fussing with matting or die cut and sticker applications. Add some renderings of places you've been and things you've seen along the way. Maps can be included to document your itinerary.

Pay special attention to the journaling process. Keep accurate details of dates and places you visit and people you meet. This is a souvenir that will send your mind traveling back in time to long, slow days of exploration and adventure.

PROJECT 27

wedding album

★★

It was the most important day of your life. The butterflies were fluttering so fiercely in your throat you could barely breath. You worried that your hair, a pampered work of art, was going to lose faith and tumble. Someone lowered the dress over your head and it slid like water down your body. Familiar hands reached to fasten those hundreds of pearl buttons.

Then there was a shout of music and, before you knew it, you were looking out over a sea of love-filled faces. Your searching eyes found that one face, that special face, and you stepped down the aisle, confident that your place was beside him.

A wedding album is a wonderful place to record your memories of those feelings. If you already have a wedding book, consider removing the photos and placing them in an acid-free environment. You'll want them to be as perfect on your 50th anniversary as they were the day they were taken.

Include a copy of your vows, the wedding invitation and the reception menu. Add your favorite love poems or verses from meaningful songs. If your wedding cake was homemade, include a copy of the recipe. Make the hours you spend creating this album a reaffirmation of your vows. Like your spouse, this is a book you will cherish forever.

Decorative corner punches add elegance to page corners. A Victorian-edged rotary cutter blade makes straight, long cuts for enhancing corner-punched shapes. Uchida®'s corner punch makes quick and easy scalloped corners. Layer small punched shapes and place randomly on the page.

PROJECT 28

tribute album

★★★

Each person who walks across the land leaves a footprint behind. Her deeds change the environment in which she lived. The children she birthed and guided and loved are living testimony to the kind of mother she was. And those lucky enough to be a part of her world were happier for having known her. Celebrate this special person with a tribute album, and the special beauty that was uniquely hers will live on forever.

A tribute album can be an on-going project or can be put together in a marathon session. It can honor a living person or be a testimonial to one who has already left this world. It should include some early photos of the honoree's life. This is a wonderful place to use that picture of the funny-looking baby in that old-fashioned pram. Work your way forward in time, chronicling with photos of your loved one in school, as a graduate, as a young mom (or dad), and as a grandparent bouncing grandchildren on the knee. Memorabilia, or shots of memorabilia, liven up the pages.

A tribute album is a wonderful gift to a special person. Tackle this project now so you and your special person can enjoy leafing through it together. Just be sure to leave spaces for all those wonderful stories that are sure to flow the first time the tribute album is read. You'll want to get them all down on paper for future generations to enjoy.

Author's note: I made this tribute album especially to honor my grandmother. When she passed away, I didn't want the world to be without her. Along with giving my grandmother a place of honor, the album gave me a place to mourn, heal and remember the joy of her life. It was lovingly and tearfully created, and therapeutic in a mysterious way.

The torn paper frame was edged with embossing ink, then dipped into gold embossing powder before heating with an embossing tool.

PROJECT 29

birthday album

★

Remember the first time you looked down on that tiny face? You were convinced that you couldn't possibly love your child more than you did at that moment. But your love grew as your child grew. With each birthday, he became more of an individual and more of a friend. A birthday album is a wonderful way to mark the progression of time and to say, "I'm so glad you're a part of my life!"

The backbone of a birthday album is all those wonderful photos of candle-blowing, gift-opening and ice cream eating. But go on and include other reminders of your child's celebration, such as party napkins, invitations, front panels of colorfully-illustrated toy packages and cake recipes.

The birthday album is a unique little project for mother and child to tackle together. When your child is very small, ask him to dictate his feelings. What was his favorite present? Who did he invite to his party and why? What's his favorite kind of birthday cake? How did he feel when everyone sang Happy Birthday? How many candles did he blow out? Then, when he's older, he can take over the journaling himself. Leave lots of room and encourage him to fill the space.

You'll find that this album project is so popular, your child will make many happy returns to these pages. Let him browse away! After all, he was the birthday boy!

Six-year-old Jason unleased artistic skills to create his own page in his birthday album. He even did his own crop-ping and left points on all the hats.

PROJECT 30

team album

★

Drive past a park on a Saturday afternoon and the sports fields will look like M&M's® packages. Kids in brightly colored uniforms will be pitching, catching, kicking and running their teams to victory. While they're concentrating on bringing home the gold, you can be concentrating on catching the best moments on film. These photos will find a perfect home in a team album.

Putting together a game-by-game book for your child's Little League team (or any other type of team) will result in BIG rewards. Include your shots, team photos, snapshots of trophies, patches, clinic schedules, tournament programs, napkins from favorite after-game pizza jaunts and team logos. Use page protectors to keep memorabilia from touching photos. Encourage players to take a few moments to write their feelings about significant plays, wins or losses on the pages. Remember to use acid-free pens.

A team album is a wonderful gift to give a favorite coach. It's sure to hit a home run every time.

*Cut-It-Up offers theme-packaged die cuts, such as sports, vacation and transportation.
Mat your photos onto first, second and third bases, as well as home plate. Use your die-cut shape for
tracing a photo template. Your child will love being the "all-star" of your life.*

PROJECT 31

quilt album

★★★★

Blessed are quilters for they are life's piece-makers. And blessed are those who discover that quilts make warm, colorful and original scrapbook albums that will warm your family's heart.

Quilt ideas and patterns are available in a wide selection of quilting books. Fiskars'® trimmer is a speedy tool that makes it easy to measure and cut rectangular, triangular or square shapes out of acid-free paper. A geometric template is another wonderful tool for this project. Take your time to play with the shapes after they've been cut, in order to find the best effect and balance.

Because quilt patterns and colors are bold, it's important to carry a design across to its facing page. Double-page spreads are strongly suggested for quilt albums in order to prevent a cluttered look. After the pages have been laid out, photos can then be placed inside select shapes.

A "stitched look" can be created by inking in thin, black dashes along the outside edges of your quilt shapes and along photos.

A quilt album is stitched together with love. Your family will happily snuggle up with this book for years to come.

Families are like quilts,
Lives pieced together,
Stitched with smiles and tears,
Colored with memories and,
Bound by love.
Heartwarming Expressions

Add some quilting quotes to bring the whole project together. Favorites include: A quilt is a blanket of love;
Memories are stitched with love; Quilts are like friends--a great source of comfort; What's stitched with love will
never tear; Happiness is... patching life's pieces together.
Not only can geometric shapes make great quilt pieces, but punched-out shapes can be used for this purpose as well.

*P*ROJECT 32

mother's journal album

★

Being a mother isn't always easy. But being a mother is always wonderful. When your heart is in maternal full-throttle, even sticky fingers and smudged walls don't seem important. After all, how can a glass of spilled milk outweigh the beauty of your child's smile or the warmth of her hug. The only bad thing about being a mother is that the years go by too quickly. Capture the moments in a mother's journal album.

This special book is an ideal place for you to record the things your child did or said that made your heart sing.

Include notes about experiences you shared. Write about your feelings. Describe the way your child looked when he belly-laughed at a knock-knock joke. Remember those words that your child couldn't seem to pronounce? "Spaghetti" came out "Getti" and "Blanket" came out "Bankie." This is a wonderful place to store those memories as well. Before you know it, your child will be grown and gone but this album will hold the childhood times near.

Children say and do the darndest things. Keep those memories alive on scrapbook pages.
Hand-cut letters can include punched shapes (notice the heart in the D). The blocks were created with a diamond-shaped template. Document on die cuts for a bit of whimsy.

PROJECT 33

hobby or collector's album

★

Bert collects paper clips and bottle caps. That's something every Sesame Street aficionado knows. He plays with them, displays them and enjoys them to the fullest. All collectors empathize with Bert's passion for collecting.

Whether you collect stamps, postcards, coins or teapots, you understand the inherent pleasure in finding, studying and looking at your collectibles. You can enjoy your hobby even more by designing a hobby or collector's album.

While paper product collectibles, stamps, cards, etc., are more easily included in an album, it is still possible to create an album of more bulky collectibles such as jewelry, china or even cars! Simply take a photo of each object in the collection.

Be sure to write about all the images included in the album and answer important questions: What history surrounds the object? What makes it special and unique? How and where did you find it?

If your album focuses on a hobby such as fishing, building model airplanes or gardening, fill the pages with photos recording your participation in the activities.

Our hobby album includes my children's many hobbies, such as fishing with their cousins at Grandpa and Grandma's house on the Minnesota Lakes. Great-Grandma Knowlen, at age 88, is always ready to clean the grandkids' fish.

Use a copy machine to enlarge die cuts to a desired size for a template. Use oversized shapes as a backdrop for photos. The Fiskar® Paper Crimper™ is a great tool for adding texture to a can of worms or fish die-cut shapes.

PROJECT 34

portrait album

★

Snapshots capture us as we are. Portraits capture us as we would like the world to see us. Before submitting to the photographer's camera, we spend hours sorting through our closets for the perfect outfit. We agonize over the right hair style, the right make up, the right accessories. And then...click! And the deed is done. The portrait has its year in a featured frame on the mantel. Then, before you know it, it's portrait time again. You find yourself faced, not only with the question of what to wear, but also with the question of what to do with last year's portrait!

Too many portraits end up backed into frames behind more current shots. There they stay, unappreciated and all but forgotten. A portrait album is a wonderful way to bring those old photographs back into view to be enjoyed. Because portraits are often large, you'll probably need an oversized album for this project. Adhere the portraits along with one or two die cuts per page. Add the names of those in the pictures and the dates, and you're done! You'll enjoy perusing these pages and seeing the evolution of all those beloved faces as both the years and the pages turn over.

PROJECT 35

sisters/friends album

★★★

You shared a comb. You shared a locker. You shared your clothes. You shared your secrets. You shared your hearts.

The special relationship between sisters or best friends, develops over many years. Through up-and-down times, this was the person you could turn to when you needed a hug or a willing ear. This is the person you could turn to when "the folks just don't understand!" Chronicle those times with a special sister or friend album.

You may have to dig to find those early photos, but it will be worth it to see your sister or friend's face light up with memories nudged by that photo of her yawning at the Girl Scout award ceremony. Include lots of stories.

Now's the time to recall incidents that seemed embarrassing when you were nine, but seem down right funny now. Leave some empty pages (if you're brave enough) so your sister or friend can add her two-cents worth.

Don't forget to include experiences you shared in your adult years. After all, the riper your friendship grew, the sweeter it became.

Sisters in the springtime,
Young, they were, and fair,
Sharing secret whisperings,
Ribbons in their hair.

As they both grew older,
Fate drew them apart.
But distance has no meaning
For the loving heart.

Kait Claire

Author's Note: Fate made us sisters…hearts made us friends. My sister-in-law, Karen, and I are best friends and kindred spirits. Pages such as this celebrate extra special relationships.
Make sure you use a safe inkpad for stamped images. Layered papers add depth to a simple design.

PROJECT 36

family tree album

★★★★★

Old black and white family photographs raise a number of questions and answer many others. You find yourself saying, "Oh, that's where my son's eyes came from!"

Ever want to be a detective? This is your chance. Historical family information can be uncovered at the library and national archives. You can find all kinds of information about your ancestors' marriages, immigrations, military records, the births of their offspring and the dates and circumstances surrounding their deaths. Old newspaper obituaries shed light on the milestones of a person's life.

Begin your album with a family tree. Include both sides of the family. Use colored photo mats and pens to differentiate between the branches. Get creative. Cut brown tree limb shapes and green leaves from paper to create a "family tree" branch that flows through the album. Try to get three or four generations on the same page. It makes it easier to trace family resemblance.

Journal richly about family members (remember to include full names, birthplace and date, plus date of death). Include information about their lives, and anecdotes about escapades and descriptions about their daily lifestyles. Pepper the pages with facts about hit movies, best-selling books, popular cars, fashion trends and social and political activity.

Don't forget to lay down your personal recollections about these people who planted the seeds and grew the roots for your own nuclear family.

*R*ESOURCE GUIDE

page ii
Canson® MiTeintes® Papercraft acid-free paper (available in fifty colors). Canson® albums; self adhesive paper shapes and adhesives. 800.628.9283.

page iii
Fiskars® punches. 715.842.2091.

page 1
Canson® acid-free paper; gold photo corners.
Personal Stamp Exchange® Live One Day at a Time" stamp (PSXG-1683) 707.588.8058.
Stampington and Company® "Musical" stamp (R-3111). 714.380.7318.
Straight Forward Stamps® texture stamp; small leaf stamp. 303.766.0536.

page 3
Provst Press's *Memory Triggering Book* by Robert M. Wendlinger. 510.845.5551.

page 4
Canson® self adhesive paper shapes. Crafty Cutter® 12" x 12" acid-free paper.

page 5
Canson® paper; self adhesive paper shapes; gold photo corners. Sakura of America® Pen-Touch Gold pen. 800.776.6257.

page 6
Most tools are resourced elsewhere except for the rubber stamps. All the rubber stamps on this page are from Personal Stamp Exchange 707.588.8058 except the *Wrought Iron Grille* stamp by Stampington & Company 714.380.9355 and the *Star Border Stamp* by Denami Design 206.639.2546. Lite Tracer Lightbox by Artograph. Doodad Rulers on Lite Tracer by C-Thru Ruler 860.243.0303. Archival Ink Pads by Ranger 732.389.3535.

page 8
TOP RIGHT:
Exposures® albums. 800.572.2502.
BOTTOM:
Canson® 3-ring binder and spiral albums.

page 9
Exposures® Ivory Brocade Wedding Album.

page 10
TOP:
Canson® self adhesive paper shapes; album; adhesive backed paper. Judi-Kins® stamp. 800.398.5834.
BOTTOM:
Hero Arts rubber stamp. 800.822.HERO Canson® shapes; paper.
Family Treasures® snowflake punch. 800.413.2645.

page 11
Canson® spiral album; adhesive backed paper; adhesive backed paper; self adhesive paper shapes.
Fiskars® Corner Edgers.™
Marvy Uchida® Metallic Gel Roller™ pen (border). 800.541.5877.
Sakura of America® Pen-Touch™ Gold pen (documentation).
C-Thru Ruler Co.® View-lers™ Ruler (border). 860.243.0303.

page 12
C-Thru Ruler Co.® View-lers™ Ruler; Déjà Views Templates™ Fiskars® Paper Edgers™ scissors. Leeco Industries® Cropper Hopper™ supply bin. 800.826.8806.

page 13
Fiskars® Paper Punch.™

page 14
Canson® albums; self adhesive paper shapes.

page 15
Satellite Publishing's *Punch Your Art Out* 800.366.6465.

page 16
Canson® acid-free paper. Fiskars® Paper Edgers™ scissors; Corner Edgers.™ Cut-It-Up® die cuts. 916.482.2288 C-Thru Ruler Co.® View-lers™ Ruler; Déjà Views™ Templates. Azadi™ Scarecrow Stamp© 800.888.3212. Marvy Uchida® LePlume Memory Series™ pens (to color stamp).

page 17
Canson® self adhesive paper shapes. Fiskars® Rotary Cutter™; Self-Healing Grid Mat™; Portable Paper Trimmer.™ C-Thru Ruler Co.® View-lers™ Ruler.

page 18
Rule-It-Up® by Cut-It-Up.®
Apple of Your Eye's *Core Composition* © by Stacy Julian and Terina Darcey. 801.582.SEED.

page 20
TOP:
EK Success, Ltd.'s *The ABC's of Creative Lettering.* 201.939.5404.
BOTTOM:
EK Success, Ltd.® Zig Memory System™ pens.

page 21
Paper Rabbit's *LMNOP; More Creative Lettering by Lindsay.* 818.957.2848.

page 22
Wasatch Mountain Design's *Lettering and Liking It; Lettering and Liking It, Too.* 801.969.1808.

page 23
425 Heartwarmin' Expressions, Vols. 1-3, by Sandra Redburn and Shelly Ehbrecht. Dist. by TweetyJill Publications. 800.595.5767.

page 24
EK Success, Ltd.® Zig Memory System™ pens.™
Rule-It-Up by Tamara Sortman; Rule-It-Up™ decorative stencil rulers. Both from Cut-It-Up.®
Page designs by Vicki Breslin.

page 25
TOP:
Paper embossing tools, stencils dist. by Family Treasures.® 800.413.2645.
BOTTOM:
Fiskars® Corner Edgers.™
McGill, Inc.® Punchline™ Punch. 815.568.7244.
Inkadinkadoo® stamp. 800.888.INKA.
EK Success, Ltd.® Zig Memory System™ pens.
Making Memories® Circle Cutter.™
Canson® adhesive backed paper shape heart. Artifacts, Inc.® Decoupage Floral Image; acid-free lace doilies. 903.729.4178.

page 27
Embossing Stylus Tool by Lasting Impressions, Lite Tracer Light Box by

Artograph 612.553.1112 and Brass Stencils by one of the following companies: Lasting Impressions, designer Kerri Hill, 801.298.1979, Heritage Handcrafts, designer Paula Hallinan 303.683.0963 and Dream Weaver, Designer Lynell Harlow 800.565.4803.

page 30
Making Memories® Circle Cutter.

pages 28 and 29
C-Thru Ruler® View-lers™ Ruler. Border designs created by designer Karen Wiessner.

page 31
Family Treasures® oval templates. Artistic Touches® vine die cut. 801.543.3372. Artifacts, Inc. acid-free heart shaped paper doilies. 903.729.4178 Canson® albums. Fiskars® Corner Edgers. McGill® Punchline™ Punch.
D.J. Inkers® rosebud paper used with permission by D.J. Hook. 801.565.0894.

page 33
Artifacts, Inc.® Decoupage Floral Design; acid-free lace doilies.
Family Treasures® stencil. Page design by Karen Wiessner.

page 35
Canson® paper. Page design by Karen Wiessner.

page 37
Family Treasures® tree punch. Artistic Touches® fishing pole die cut.

page 41
McGill® silhouette heart punch. Paper Patch® paper. 801.253.3018. Artistic Albums & More® gingerbread man die cut. 888.9.ALBUMS.

page 43
Ellison® die cuts: music note, stars (©™) 800.253.2238
McGill® Punchline™ rectangular punch.

page 45
Fiskars® Paper Edgers™ scissors. Family Treasures® Jumbo Series™ scissors.

page 47
Canson® albums, paper.

page 49
Ideas for page layouts by designer Jenny Friedman.

page 51
Canson® albums.

page 53
Canson® albums; adhesive backed paper shapes.

page 55
Artistic Touches® baby block die cut. Udderly Yours® die cuts. 602.545.8777 Paper Patch® printed paper. Artifacts, Inc.® acid-free paper doilies. C-Thru Ruler Co.® View-lers™ Ruler. McGill® heart punch.

page 57
Canson® albums.

page 59
Exposures® albums.

page 63
Ellison® tree (©™) die cuts.

page 65
Canson® self adhesive paper shapes. Page title design from Wasatch Mtn. Design's *Lettering and Liking It.*

page 67
All Night Media, Inc.® rubber stamps. 800.STAMPED.
Canson® black photo corners. Artistic Touches® skyline border die cut. Judi-Kins® postage stamp. 800.398.5834

page 69
Crafty Cutter® paper (handcut tree shape). Ellison® anchor. (©™)
Fiskars® Wave Paper Edger.™

page 71
Ellison® star (©™) die cut.

page 73
Canson® self adhesive paper shapes. Ellison® large apple (©™) die cuts. McGill® punches.
Crafty Cutter® paper (handcut world, blackboard, pencil).

page 75
Canson® paper, gold corners. Hero Arts® Sun Flower stamp. Rubber Stampede® leaf stamp, spiral and crosses. 800.632.8386. Family Treasures® Mini Victorian Scissor.™

page 77
Canson® paper; albums; self adhesive paper shapes.

page 79
Exposures® albums.

page 81
McGill® hearts corner punch. Fiskars® Rotary Cutter™ with Tiara™ blade. Family Treasures®heart punches. Uchida® Scallop Corner Rounder.™

page 83
Personal Stamp Exchange® love block of four stamps; gold embossing powder. 707.588.8058.
Wildlife Enterprises, Ltd.® stamp. 530.626.5924.
Canson® album; paper; gold photo corners.

page 87
Crafty Cutter® paper. Cut-It-Out® theme die cuts. Making Memories® circle cutter.

page 89
McGill® long reach, flower, heart punches. Saying from *425 More Heartwarmin' Expressions.*
Paper Patch® printed papers. Crafty Cutter® solid colored paper.

page 91
Ellison® die cut fire truck. Family Treasures® Geometric Template. McGill® heart punch.

page 93
Ellison® die cuts: small fish (©™), fish (enlarged).
Fiskars® Paper Crimper™ made crimped designs.
Canson® die cuts.

page 95
Canson® paper and shapes.

page 97
Personal Stamp Exchange® "The Best of Times"™ stamp; Aspen Leaf™ stamp.

page 99
Canson® bow shapes; paper. Frames hand torn against a ruler. Sakura of America® Pen-Touch Gold.™

page 102
Canson® photo.

Now you have the resources–
so get started!

Persistence and energy conquer all things.
Benjamin Franklin

I'll note you in my book of memory.
William Shakespeare